Who Am I?

Psychological exercises
to develop self-understanding

Published in 2018 by The School of Life
First published in the USA in 2020
930 High Road, London, N12 9RT

Copyright © The School of Life 2018

Designed and typeset by Marcia Mihotich
Printed in China by Leo Paper Group

A proportion of this book has appeared online at
www.theschooloflife.com/articles

The School of Life publishes a range of books on essential topics in
psychological and emotional life, including relationships, parenting,
friendship, careers and fulfilment. The aim is always to help us to
understand ourselves better – and thereby to grow calmer, less confused
and more purposeful. Discover our full range of titles, including books
for children, here:
www.theschooloflife.com/books

The School of Life also offers a comprehensive therapy service,
which complements, and draws upon, our published works:
www.theschooloflife.com/therapy

ISBN 978-1-912891-08-5

10 9

Contents

1
Psychology

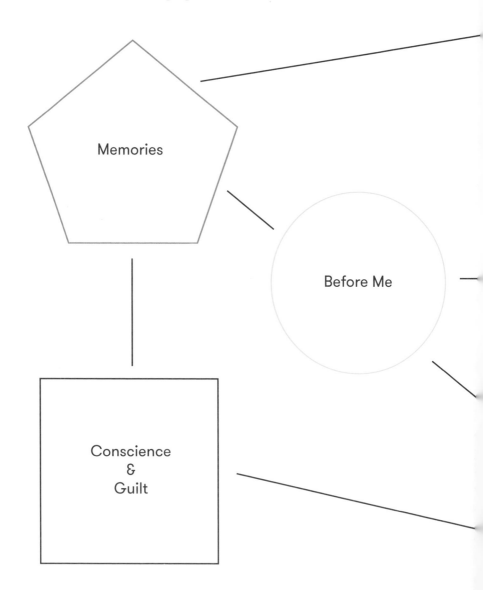

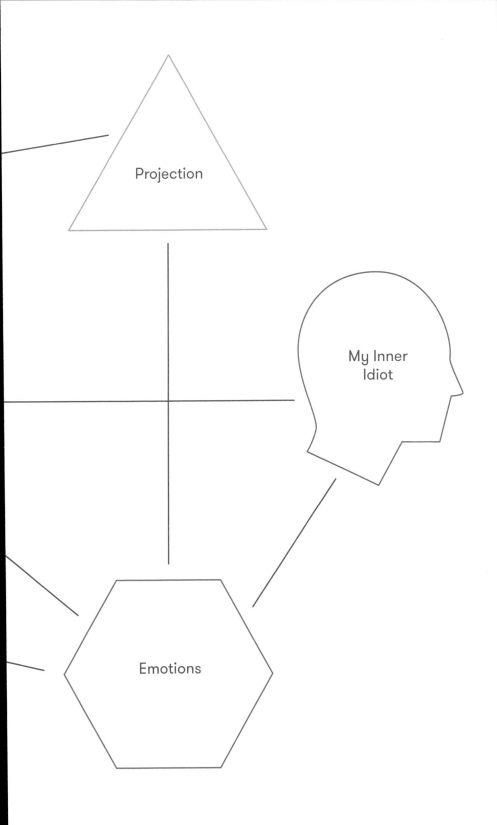

Projection

My Inner
Idiot

Emotions

1   Before I was born

'We' began long before we were actually conceived. Our characters are deeply tied to aspects of our parents' lives that they may have been coy about discussing directly.

What was your mother like as a teenager?

....

....

....

....

....

....

....

And your father?

....

....

....

....

....

....

Imagine your mother or father with their mother or father: what might the emotional atmosphere have been like?

....

....

....

....

....

....

....

2   Me in history

We enter history through a very particular door: a class, an economy, a moment in the history of manners and fashion, a particular position in every nation's perpetual swing between hope and despair.

What was the corner of the world like into which you tumbled? And its mood?

....
....
....
....
....
....
....
....
....
....

How might this have marked you?

....
....
....
....
....
....
....
....
....
....
....

3   Blame

All parents make enormous mistakes. Our individualities are born from them.
We are in large measure the sum of our parents' errors.

What did yours do wrong?

....
....
....
....
....
....
....
....
....
....

Why – do we imagine – did they mess up, assuming that they were not
simply being deliberately nasty? What sufferings of their own made them less
than ideal?

....
....
....
....
....
....
....
....
....
....
....
....
....

4　How did my parents get on?

The way our parents behaved towards one another gives us an enduring notion of what all relationships might be like.

What were your parents like together at their best?

And at their worst?

5   My bedroom when I was a child

It will probably have been a place of intense emotion, in which much that was fascinating and some of what was sorrowful unfolded.

Sketch the room, including as many details as possible.

....

....

Add a little more detail:

Was it usually quite messy or tidy?

....

....

....

....

....

What were three favourite toys?

....

....

....

....

....

What were the nicest times of day in that room?

....

....

....

....

....

What do you miss about that time?

....

....

....

....

....

....

6   Sensory memories of childhood

Childhood is filled with intense sensory experiences. It's not always so much actual events that stick in our minds, but little details: smells, lights, textures of carpet, types of foods... They are the guardians of our past.

Name some foods that retain powerful emotional atmospheres from childhood.

....
....
....
....
....
....
....

When you were on the floor, what kind of material, temperature and feel was it?

....
....
....
....
....
....
....

Where did you feel cosy?

....
....
....
....
....
....

What are the times of day (and night) that still now take you back to childhood?

....

....

....

....

....

....

....

....

Was there a place you went to when you felt sad?

....

....

....

....

....

....

....

....

Did you ever feel awe: a sense of the majesty, mystery and scale of the universe?
Where were you when that happened?

....

....

....

....

....

....

....

....

7   Projection

The way we see the world is profoundly influenced by our past experience. We bring this experience to bear on the present almost without noticing, in a process that psychologists call 'projection'.

A classic projection test is 'the unfinished sentence', which, as we complete it, summons up bits of our assumptions and childhood legacies we might otherwise never have accessed.

Crucially, we shouldn't think too much when completing the sentences, so as to allow our unconscious to be surprised and say exactly what is on its mind.

What I really deserve is...

....

....

....

....

....

Deep down, I suppose I'm really...

....

....

....

....

....

Men are generally...

....

....

....

....

....

Women almost always...

....
....
....
....
....
....

What I really want to say to other people is...

....
....
....
....
....
....

When someone disappoints me, I...

....
....
....
....
....

If someone else could know me properly, they'd...

....
....
....
....
....

You can do a similar game with paintings:
Botticelli – *Mother and Child*

What's she thinking?

How does the baby feel?

What is he
thinking about?

What might happen next?

What might his love life be like?

Gustave Caillebotte – *Man on Balcony*

Without worrying at all about historical reality, look at the
picture and imagine:

....
....
....
....
....
....
....
....
....
....
....
....
....
....
....
....
....
....
....
....
....
....
....
....
....
....
....
....
....
....
....
....
....

Titian – *The Three Ages of Man*

We bring so much intimate history and personality into our answers and interpretations. We don't need to stop projecting, and can't either, but it can help to get more aware of our tendencies to interpret the world in very particular ways because of the distinctive timbre of our past.

....

....

....

....

....

....

....

....

....

....

....

....

....

....

....

....

....

....

....

....

....

....

....

What's she feeling
and thinking?

What's he feeling
and thinking?

8   Sunday evening

We are slightly different versions of ourselves at different times. Sunday evening can be the time of the week when all the demands and social duties are done: it's peaceful, nicely empty; or maybe it's dominated by the looming approach of Monday morning. The weekend is already over and gone; perhaps it's a time when you miss certain people or remember some of the sweeter things of childhood.

What thoughts are often going through your mind on a Sunday evening?

....

....

....

....

....

....

....

....

....

....

....

....

....

....

....

....

....

....

....

....

....

9   Conscience and guilt

For many centuries, conscience was thought of in religious terms as a moral voice - stemming from God - in our heads, judging the goodness or badness of our actions and intentions. It would lead us to feel guilty when we transgressed and sometimes prompt us to do the right thing when there was a chance.

How active is your conscience?

....

....

....

....

....

....

....

What makes you feel guilty?

....

....

....

....

....

....

....

....

What do you rather easily allow yourself to get away with?

....

....

....

....

....

....

....

10   Inner voices

It's a strange but central phenomenon: we sometimes talk silently to ourselves in voices that are internalised versions of voices we once heard around us (those of mothers, fathers, friends, colleagues, etc.). We make comments on our own conduct: we call ourselves a fool or a waster, we reassure and treat ourselves – and as we do so, we take on an accent that once came from someone outside of us. It might be the words of a harassed or angry parent that we're recycling, or the menacing threats of an older sibling keen to put us down, or a grandmother who was kindly and always encouraging. These powerful past figures live on in our heads.

Let's audit some of our inner voices.

Whose are the constructive, kindly voices in your head?

....

....

....

....

....

....

....

....

....

....

....

....

....

....

....

....

....

....

Imagine that a negative inner voice could be replaced by a wiser, more generous and more intelligent one. What would it sound like?

....
....
....
....
....
....
....
....
....
....
....
....

Whose are the punitive, scolding, mocking voices?

....
....
....
....
....
....
....
....
....
....
....

11 Self-love

How much do you like yourself?

....
....
....
....
....
....
....
....

Who taught you to be kind to yourself?

....
....
....
....
....
....
....
....
....

How were you taught to be suspicious of, and attack, yourself?

....
....
....
....
....
....
....
....

12   Sulking

How hard is it for you to talk to loved ones when you are upset and explain clearly and calmly what is up?

Over what sort of things do you sulk?

....

....

....

....

....

....

....

....

....

....

....

....

Why did you fail to learn to express yourself directly, with confidence?

....

....

....

....

....

....

....

....

....

....

....

13 Compliance

To what extent do you have to be a good boy or girl?

....
....
....
....
....
....
....
....

What or who in the past forced a high degree of compliance on you?

....
....
....
....
....
....
....
....

If you were freed from the imperative to be so 'good', what might you do?

....
....
....
....
....
....
....
....
....

14   Anger

What gets you into a rage?

If, beneath the anger, there is often fear, what are you very afraid of?

15 Trust

Does the world feel safe, more or less?

....

....

....

....

....

....

....

Can you expect to get justice?

....

....

....

....

....

....

Can catastrophe suddenly descend from nowhere?

....

....

....

....

....

....

Who shaped your degree of trust?

....

....

....

....

....

....

16   Evolution

We all want to evolve in some way, though here the topic is not so much external change – like making more money, getting on better at work or toning our body – as internal evolution.

What sort of things might you wish to change about yourself?

....
....
....
....
....
....
....
....
....
....
....
....
....

What would it mean to grow up a little more?

....
....
....
....
....
....
....
....
....
....
....
....

17   Addictions

Addiction is a manic reliance on something, anything, to keep our darker or more unsettling thoughts and feelings at bay. The key thing isn't what we're addicted to – it could be pretty much anything, and might even sound rather innocuous to others: scanning the news, learning Italian, cleaning the house, sending witty messages to our friends. What matters is that we use these things relentlessly to block engagement with thoughts we don't like having – but that are, sadly, ones we need to pay attention to.

What things do you turn to in order to block out feelings and ideas?

....

....

....

....

....

....

....

....

....

What are the tricky feelings and ideas you've little wish to experience?

....

....

....

....

....

....

....

....

....

....

....

18 Reminders to ourselves

There are a host of fundamental lessons we know we should heed, but never quite do. We would ideally write them up on the wall, so as to see them every hour. Perhaps we should be working harder or thinking more or attempting to expand our experiences.

What ideas should we in particular keep reminding ourselves of in order to improve our lives and grow into our better selves?

19   My inner idiot

We don't necessarily enjoy admitting it to others (or to ourselves), but in more candid moments we can accept that we are, in multiple ways, a bit of an idiot. We're clumsy, we get worked up about ridiculous things, we say regrettable words, we make stupid spur-of-the-moment decisions and commitments, we fritter our time away. Detailing our own inner idiot isn't an exercise in self-contempt; it's an attempt to look head-on at a spectre we normally try to deny exists.

What are some of the things you feel very embarrassed about doing and being?

....
....
....
....
....
....
....
....
....

When is your inner idiot active?

....
....
....
....
....
....
....
....
....
....

20 Nostalgia

Sometimes we catch ourselves drawn powerfully to some past period –
childhood, ten years ago in Italy... Or a time we feel we'd quite like to have
lived in – the late 18th century, Rome under the rule of Marcus Aurelius... Such a
daydream is circling something that's missing in our lives, something that we feel
we can't easily get in the present.

What triggers your nostalgia?

What might your nostalgia be trying to tell you?

21 My (relatively) imminent death

It's a hateful yet crucial thought. We know we're mortal, but we keep this knowledge firmly in the background. Taking our own death seriously isn't morbid: it invites us to a wiser sense of our priorities now.

Given how short life is, what should you do now?

....

....

....

....

....

....

....

....

....

....

....

....

....

....

....

....

....

....

....

....

....

....

....

....

....

22 Headlines

There are news outlets that make a speciality of summing up a person, and their life, in an excoriating headline: 'posh druggie jumps under a train'; 'shopaholic doctor's wife has affair'. But these stories could be told very differently. In fact they have been: in *Anna Karenina* and *Madame Bovary*, Tolstoy and Flaubert transformed such headlines, which they had read in the press, into the most compassionate and tender novels of the 19th century. Painfully, we tend – at difficult moments – to describe ourselves to ourselves with the abbreviated cruelty of a scandalous headline: 'loser loses'; 'weak idiot taken advantage of once again'.

Here on the left are some headline self-criticisms and, on the right, some kinder and truer statements.

Cruel headline	Novelistic (kinder) telling of the story
They were so arrogant	Ideas excited them, they wanted others to share their enthusiasms, they spoke passionately, with conviction; at times they got carried away...
They never stepped out of their parents' shadow	The deep tension between love and independence was never fully resolved; it was difficult...
Uptight, bad-tempered	Dignity is so fragile, yet so important; they longed for warmth and tenderness, but...
Boring	They struggled to convey to others all the inward movements of their complex soul...
Idiot	Yes, the opportunity was there, but it was hard to identify at the time; for a million reasons their fears got the better of them; they felt...

What horrible headline might you be tempted to give to your own life?

....
....
....
....
....
....
....
....
....
....
....
....
....

Now try to retell it nicely, compassionately, with sympathy and generosity.

....
....
....
....
....
....
....
....
....
....
....
....
....
....
....
....

2
Relationships

1   What I first learned about love

Our first experience of loving and being loved occurred when we were children. A parent's love may at times be deeply tender and enchanting – but it can easily involve tricky dynamics as well. Perhaps we learned to love a depressed parent, or a very irritable one. Perhaps we came to associate love with trying very hard to please or a constant fear of abandonment; we might have been exposed to favouritism, and learned to see love as something we could only get if another person didn't. A parent might have conveyed the impression that they could only love us if we were very good, or if we remained docile and dependent – suggesting that independent successes of our own would signal the end of their love for us.

What might have been less than ideal in your childhood experience of love?

....
....
....
....
....
....
....
....

How might the themes you have identified in childhood love still be showing up in your adult love experiences?

....
....
....
....
....
....
....
....

2 What unhealthy things feel attractive in a partner?

Because whom we love as adults mirrors the emotions we felt in love as children, we may find ourselves powerfully drawn to partners not just for their positive qualities but also, more darkly, for their capacity to make us suffer in ways that feel enticingly familiar.

What tricky character traits do you find yourself being drawn to?

....
....
....
....
....
....

How are these similar to those of a parental figure?

....
....
....
....
....
....

What varieties of emotional health turn you off?

....
....
....
....
....
....

3   Avoidant and anxious attachment

Psychologists like to divide us into 'avoidant' and 'anxious' kinds of lovers. An avoidant pattern of relating to lovers means that, when there is difficulty, we grow cold and distant, and deny our need for anyone. We desperately want to be reassured but feel so anxious that we may be unwanted, we disguise our need behind a façade of indifference. At the precise moment when we want to be close, we say we're busy, we pretend our thoughts are elsewhere, we get sarcastic and dry; we imply that a need for reassurance would be the last thing on our minds. We might even have an affair, the ultimate face-saving attempt to be distant – and often a perverse attempt to assert that we don't require a partner's love (that we have been too reserved to ask for).

For its part, anxious attachment is a pattern of relating to lovers whereby, when there is difficulty, we grow officious, procedural and controlling over small matters of domestic routine.

We feel our partners are escaping us emotionally, but rather than admitting our sense of loss, we respond by trying to pin them down administratively. We get unduly cross that they are eight minutes late, we chastise them heavily for not having done certain chores, we ask them strictly if they've completed a task they had agreed vaguely to undertake. All this rather than admit the truth: 'I'm worried that I don't matter to you...'.

Are you more anxious or more avoidant in your attachment style?

....
....
....
....
....
....
....

Describe a recent episode of either type of attachment playing itself out.

....
....
....
....
....
....
....

How do you think you acquired yours?

....
....
....
....
....
....
....

4   My difficulties

We don't usually feel we're difficult, but we are. So many things strike us as obviously necessary or obviously unimportant – but it's hard for us to see just how differently they might appear to another person.

Imagine a candid friend who knows you well explaining to someone else how you might be a difficult person to live with day to day. What sorts of things might they point out?

....

....

....

....

....

....

....

....

....

....

What kind of forgiveness would another person need to deploy to cope with your tricky sides?

....

....

....

....

....

....

....

....

....

....

5   Lessons from old relationships

Ideally, from every relationship we learn something important about ourselves – about our own failings, perhaps, or about a tendency to ignore warning signals.

Jot down a list of all the people you've had relationships with – even if these unions were quite brief.

....
....
....
....
....
....
....
....
....
....

What did you learn about yourself?

....
....
....
....
....
....
....
....
....
....
....

What criticisms of you might these past lovers make?

How would you behave if you could turn back the clock?

6   Deepest desires

What would you ideally want your partner properly to understand about you?

7   Little things

We can get deeply upset over what can seem to be tiny details: it's essential to use a breadboard when cutting bread – or maybe it's completely unnecessary; the dishes must be clean before eating – or is this a cold imposition? We can be driven to despair by the way our partner says a particular word too often or by the way they blow their nose or brush their teeth. It feels so shameful to get bothered about such apparently trivial things.

To understand ourselves better we need to explore – as calmly as we can – why it is these little details matter so much to us. They are always symbols of bigger issues: a troubling attitude to existence in general seems to be condensed into an inability to close a drawer properly or into a tendency to giggle.

What small things annoy you in a partner?

....
....
....
....
....
....
....

What is the bigger story behind your intense reactions?

....
....
....
....
....
....
....
....
....

8 Rows

It's inevitable that there will be conflict in a relationship – since it's deeply improbable that two separate people will see eye to eye on everything that matters to them. We get so caught up in the intensity of the conflict that it's tricky to observe that we are, at heart, scared – scared that someone in whom we have invested so much is failing to understand issues of primordial importance to us.

What deeply significant things does your partner have a tendency not to understand?

....
....
....
....
....
....
....
....
....
....
....
....
....
....
....
....
....
....
....
....
....
....

9   Apologising

It's impossible that we never do anything that upsets our partner. The function of an apology is to let them know that we understand that we've hurt them – and to signal that we're genuinely sorry about this. But we often don't apologise because it feels too dangerous to admit the guilt we actually feel: we'll have to back down on too much that we still care about. It feels too one-sided. And so our partner thinks we don't notice or don't care about the pain and distress we've caused them.

What, ideally, would you like to apologise about to your partner?

....

....

....

....

....

....

....

....

....

....

What do you worry would happen if you did?

....

....

....

....

....

....

....

....

....

10   Secrets in love

Our Romantic culture makes it feel as if secrets are the enemy of love: those who love should share every detail of their thoughts and actions. What's your attitude to this? In reality, we might feel we need to protect our partner from a few facts about us that they might, understandably, misunderstand in a disastrous way.

What do you hide from your partner?

....
....
....
....
....
....
....
....
....

What do you think they might be hiding from you?

....
....
....
....
....
....
....
....
....
....
....
....
....

11   Wanting my partner to change

To seek to change one's lover feels like a profound offence against the whole idea of love because we often think that love means thinking a person is perfect as they already are. By contrast, there's another – less Romantic, more Classical – view that sees love as an arena of growth and change. This view of love was developed in Ancient Greece, prompted particularly by the philosophical ideas of Socrates and Plato. As they saw it, the task of love is first and foremost to educate one's lover. We don't love someone because we think they are perfect already but because we can see what they could be; we love their potential and their emergent (but not yet fully developed) qualities. Their deep attachment to us means that we have an ideal opportunity for guiding and shaping their development towards the articulation of their full potential. Love is a mutually supportive structure in which two people can guide each other to their respective virtuous ideal selves. But the ancient philosophers were clear: we have to get the other to want to change, not by criticising them, but by making change feel appealing.

What would you like to change in your partner?

....
....
....
....

How do you currently go about it?

....
....
....
....

What could make this change feel attractive (and not just a burdensome demand) to your partner?

....
....
....
....

12   Being changed by my partner

In our more honest moods, we admit we're far from perfect as we are. But very understandably we resent heavy-handed lessons.

Ideally, what would you like to learn from your partner?

....
....
....
....
....
....
....

And how could they best teach you? How would the lesson need to be delivered?

....
....
....
....
....
....
....

What do you need to be teased about?

....
....
....
....
....
....
....

13 How I need help to be delivered

When we've got a problem, our partner might want to help us if they can. But the intention to be helpful isn't all that matters. It also matters how the help is being offered. There are a few main options.

- Being listened to
- Being offered solutions
- Hearing an optimistic prognosis
- Hearing a pessimistic prognosis
- Being offered cuddles

Which do you prefer?

....
....
....
....
....
....
....
....
....

Which do you really not like?

....
....
....
....
....
....
....
....
....

3
Sex

1   What's erotic for me?

Often our first instinct is to think about what we're attracted to in terms of overt bodily features, but our excitement around another person is frequently connected to less obvious things: a glance, a manner of speaking, a special tone of voice, whispering, someone who is going to lead us astray – or someone reserved who needs a lot of artful seduction.

What are your erotic fantasies and concerns?

....

....

....

....

....

....

....

....

....

....

....

....

....

....

....

....

....

....

....

....

....

....

....

2   Explaining a desire to another person

We often worry that something we'd like to do will sound strange to another person – we fear their reaction. But what another person might accept isn't usually precisely defined: it might depend quite a lot on how we approach the topic and how we make sense of this desire for them. It's not simply whether they'll want to do it, but the fear that they'll think we're bizarre or crazy or just not very nice. So we have to build up a portrait of why our erotic imagination works the way it does.

What desires do you have that you worry another person might think are odd?

....
....
....
....
....

How could you ideally explain them to a partner?

....
....
....
....
....

How did this interest develop?

....
....
....
....

How does it link up with other bits of your character?

....
....
....
....

3   Resistance

Sigmund Freud's great insight was that many things remain unconscious because of our impulse toward what he called 'resistance'. The unconscious contains desires and feelings that deeply challenge a more comfortable vision of ourselves. But the price of not facing up to them is anxiety and neurosis. We should make peace with our glorious oddities and contradictions.

What sexual activities or experiences might you feel ambivalent about (because they conflict with your avowed orientation, belief system or sense of self), but might secretly have a certain appeal?

4   Sex as therapy

The sexual scenarios that excite us don't just occur by chance. In a disguised but important way, they often present ideal solutions to troublesome issues in our lives.

Issue	What I like sexually	The therapeutic idea
Nervous around authority	A partner who takes control	Authority can be exciting, not just a threat
I might be domineering and controlling, fussy and demanding	A partner who likes being more passive	I can be strong and my partner can really enjoy that and not resent it
I feel I need to be very polite all the time	Talking dirty in bed	One can say something very rude, and the other person isn't offended – in fact, they're delighted
I always have to preserve my dignity	Making a mess, being very playful and silly around sex	One can do things that would otherwise seem ridiculous or embarrassing, but the other likes you for it

What might your list look like?

Issue	What I like sexually	The therapeutic idea

5   Normality

It's usually pretty important to us to feel that we're normal – not too far out of the range of ideas and desires that would make sense to other people. But we're not actually very good at gauging what other people are really like, since we almost always encounter an edited, limited version of who they are, which is rather misleading in certain ways. So we often construct a disturbing view of ourselves as far odder in a statistical sense than we really are.

What do you feel might be quite odd about you sexually?
(Imagine if it wasn't really so odd.)

6   Sex and love

Mostly, in our society, it is taken for granted that sex and love ought to be very closely connected. But this hasn't always and everywhere been the case. There are and have been societies where it didn't seem particularly logical or necessary to think that sex is tied to marriage or to long-term love. In 18th-century Venice, marriage was hugely important, who you married was a crucial decision, weddings were lavishly celebrated, divorce was almost impossible, but it was considered normal for each married partner to have lovers.

How closely are love and sex linked for you? And why?
(This isn't about changing your behaviour but about exploring what you think.)

....
....
....
....
....
....
....
....
....
....
....
....
....
....
....
....
....
....
....
....

4
Other People

1   Imaginary speeches

There are so many things we want to say to certain people that we don't, for fear of causing offence or prompting an unhelpful retaliation. Nevertheless, often late at night or in the early morning, we run imaginary speeches in our minds – and gain relief from doing so. When we think of the content of such speeches, we might imagine that they would be about anger or hurt that we hadn't been able to communicate properly – but they could just as well be about a muffled tenderness, compassion or love.

Who are some of the people you haven't been able to say the important things to – and what is it you would ideally say? Sketch a few of the ideal speeches.

2   Irritations

We are as much defined by the people we dislike and who annoy us as we are by those we admire and love. Think over the people you have known and taken against. Generalise outwards from particular examples to a broader underlying value system, comprising at least five themes.

What traits do you dislike most in people?

....
....
....
....
....
....
....
....
....
....
....
....
....
....
....
....
....
....
....
....
....

3   Those you have been mean to

We are often deeply ashamed of those we have been less than nice towards.
Yet we all have such characters in our pasts. Rather than dismiss thoughts
of them with shame, think back to what really happened with them. More
particularly, reinterpret your own meanness as stemming not so much from evil
as from a kind of anxiety that deserves to be better understood.

What kind of worries drove on your less admirable moments around other
people? List the people involved, and the fears that powered your behaviour.

....

....

....

....

....

....

....

....

....

....

....

....

....

....

....

....

....

....

....

....

....

....

....

....

4   Loneliness

We are often ashamed of feeling lonely, but a high degree of loneliness is an inexorable part of being a sensitive, intelligent human. It's a built-in feature of a complex existence. A few others might understand us in part, but much of who we really are will elude even them.

What makes you feel lonely? What do you wish others could understand but – despite your best efforts – don't so much?

....

....

....

....

....

....

....

....

....

....

What would you now want to tell an ideal imaginary friend?

....

....

....

....

....

....

....

....

....

....

....

5   Friendship

If we have an ambitious view of friendship, we'll probably feel we don't have a sufficient number of truly good friends. The word 'friend' is in part to blame, covering everything from a casual connection to someone we feel powerfully close to in important ways.

What character traits would you need in an ideally good friend?

....

....

....

....

....

What sides of you should they appreciate?

....

....

....

....

....

What vulnerabilities could you share with this person that you'd not normally disclose to others?

....

....

....

....

....

What would you not mind much in them that otherwise could be a bit annoying?

....

....

....

....

6   Enemies

It's very disconcerting to think that someone actively wishes us ill. An enemy wants to humiliate us or make us look stupid.

How do you react? Panic or relative calm?

....

....

....

....

....

What do you think motivates them? Are they right or peculiar to hate you?

....

....

....

....

....

What might have gone wrong for them in the past that they are taking out on you now?

....

....

....

....

....

Name five of your biggest enemies across your life (even back to school)? Do they have anything in common in their accusations?

....

....

....

....

....

7 Boasting

We are, by dint of good socialisation, probably very scared of boasting. We take care to downplay our positive sides and to be modest about our achievements. But it can help to let our basic (and healthy) reserves of egoism have their say every now and then.

In what ways are we, in a sense, rather fabulous? What terrific sides of us does the world too readily ignore?

....

....

....

....

....

....

....

....

....

....

Who or what has made us very shy about not doing anything that sounds like boasting?

....

....

....

....

....

....

....

....

....

....

....

8 Beauty and ugliness

We are rarely utterly convinced of our total ugliness or beauty: we veer in our assessment, often because of what we feel emotionally. Our looks stay more or less stable, but there are days when we feel distinctly ugly – and others when we're alive to our more attractive qualities.

What is ugly in our features?

....

....

....

....

....

....

....

....

....

....

....

In what ways can we be, despite everything, sometimes, a bit attractive?

....

....

....

....

....

....

....

....

....

....

....

....

9   The weaknesses of our strengths

Every strength that an individual has necessarily brings with it a weakness of which it is a devilish part. It is impossible to have strengths without weaknesses. Every virtue has an associated 'vice'. A person's qualities in one area necessarily give rise to problematic dimensions elsewhere. For example, the discipline and rigour that make a person good at managing a budget can also make them a difficult travelling companion; the playfulness and easy-going tolerance that makes someone delightful at a party can render them slovenly and heedless about household chores. Strength of character and bravery can lead to emotional reserve and uncomfortable invulnerability.

The idea invites us to look with greater tolerance on certain failings in ourselves and to consider the relationship between our strong and weak sides.

Fill out the table that connects up your strengths with your weaknesses:

My strengths	The 'weaknesses' they give rise to

5
Work

1   Parental expectations

Modern parents will always say that they don't care what their children do, so long as they are happy. This is rarely exactly true. In small ways and large, parents shape our professional expectations. It starts with what parents understand of the working world.

What sorts of jobs did your parents understand – and respect?

....

....

....

What jobs were frightening or simply alien to them?

....

....

....

....

In what ways have you honoured your parents' wishes?

....

....

....

....

In what ways have you rebelled against your parents' wishes?

....

....

....

....

If it wasn't for parental expectations, what might you do/have done?

....

....

....

....

2   Fantasy jobs

There are so many good reasons why certain jobs are impractical; that doesn't stop them being a vibrant and legitimate part of our fantasy life. They are 'our' jobs too in a way. By fantasy, we don't mean entirely unrealistic, we mean sincerely connected up to bits of our characters, but out of reach for a variety of regrettable yet understandable reasons.

Given who you are, what should you ideally be doing?

....

....

....

....

....

....

....

....

....

Name three jobs to which you would be well suited but that are practically speaking beyond you, given life as it is?

....

....

....

....

....

....

....

....

....

....

....

....

....

3   Childhood

What we liked to do, and play, as children gives us vital clues as to our true working selves. It's when we had no thought of money or status that our real interests had a chance to come to the fore. Clues as to our true working destiny may, surprisingly, lie back at a time when we were not thinking of work at all.

What did you enjoy playing as a child?

....

....

....

....

....

....

....

....

....

....

If you took your childhood interests seriously, and translated them into their adult idioms, what might you be doing?

....

....

....

....

....

....

....

....

....

....

....

4   Ambitions

Any working life involves a balance between worldly and authentic concerns;
a balancing act between what the world requires and what we like.

Rank in order of importance for you in your career:
Money, Status, Creativity, Social Impact, Colleagues.

....
....
....
....
....
....
....
....
....
....

What do you hope for in each area?

....
....
....
....
....
....
....
....
....
....
....

5 Meaning

We work for money and status, of course, but we also work for something a little more mysterious: meaning. What makes a job meaningful is usually the degree to which we can see how what we're doing contributes to increasing the pleasures of others or reducing their suffering. Often what we do actually does make a contribution – it's just that the chain of connections is quite long or complicated and we don't see the detailed results in other people's lives. So a job might feel less meaningful than it really is: the supermarket logistics manager isn't there when an eleven-year-old takes their first tentative steps in preparing a meal for their parents.

In what way is your job meaningful?

....
....
....
....
....
....
....
....
....
....

How could you insert more of a sense of meaning into your working life?

....
....
....
....
....
....
....
....
....
....

6 . Envy

Nice people aren't supposed to feel envy very much: it feels rather embarrassing, greedy and immature. Yet envy is a very natural response to the fact that others have good things, or good qualities, that we don't yet possess. The ideal isn't simply to suffer envy but to learn from it. Envy provides a clue to who we really want to be – though the meaning of the clue might not be immediately obvious.

Name some people that you envy – and define why.

....

....

....

....

....

....

....

....

....

....

....

With your envious feelings in mind, how could you try to reform your life?

....

....

....

....

....

....

....

....

....

....

7   Evolution, not revolution

When we think of 'changing our lives', we often picture a dramatic transformation. We imagine leaving a job, returning to education, suffering a vast drop in income and so on. No wonder, conceived of in these terms, we often don't change anything. But there could be another way of changing our lives, through a process of small branching moves that don't upset the essential tenor of our lives (or at least not for a while).

What small, unfrightening steps might you take in the coming days to change the direction of your career?

....

....

....

....

....

....

....

....

....

....

....

....

....

....

....

....

....

....

....

....

8 If you could not fail...

Given the hold that the fear of failure has on our imaginations, it can help to ask that vast and essential question:

If you could not fail, what would you do?

....
....
....
....
....
....
....
....
....
....
....
....
....
....
....
....
....
....
....
....
....
....
....
....
....
....
....

9   Fixation

A Job Fixation is a determination to secure a particular kind of job which – for one reason or another – turns out not to be a promising or realistic option. It may be that the job is extremely difficult to attain, it may require long years of preparation or it might be in an industry that has become precarious and therefore denies us good long-term prospects.

We call it a fixation – rather than simply an interest – to signal that the focus on the job is proving problematic because we have an overwhelming sense that our future lies with this one occupation and this occupation alone – while nevertheless facing a major obstacle in turning our idea into a reality. The solution to such fixations lies in coming to understand more closely what we are really interested in, because the more accurately and precisely we fathom what we really care about, the more we stand to discover that our interests actually exist in a far broader range of occupations than we have until now been used to entertaining.

The careful investigation of what we love in one field of work shows us – paradoxically but liberatingly – that we could in fact also love working in a slightly different field.

What job might you be guilty of fixating on getting?

....
....
....
....
....
....
....
....

What are the qualities you like in this job?

....
....
....
....
....
....
....
....
....
....

Where else in the job market might these qualities be utilised and required?

....
....
....
....
....
....
....
....
....

10 Impostor syndrome

Around many personal and professional tasks we're held back by the odd-sounding, but very real, feeling that we are 'impostors', that we're somehow tricking others into thinking that we have abilities and capacities we actually lack. And we get very worried that we're going to be found out. Others will realise how confused, uninspired, lazy or unsophisticated we really are – and we'll be humiliated.

In what way do we feel like impostors in our work?

....
....
....
....
....
....
....
....
....
....

Who in our past might have helped (perhaps entirely unwittingly) to foster our sense of ourselves as impostors?

....
....
....
....
....
....
....
....
....
....
....

11   Self-Sabotage

It's normal to expect that we will always – almost by nature – actively seek out our own happiness in relationships and careers. Yet we often act as if we were deliberately out to ruin our chances. When going on dates, we may lapse into unnecessarily opinionated and antagonistic behaviour. In relationships, we may drive well-intentioned partners to distraction through repeated unwarranted accusations and angry explosions. At work, we may stumble before the biggest chances.

Such behaviour can't always be put down to mere bad luck. It may deserve a stronger, more intentional term: self-sabotage. We destroy our opportunities because of a background sense that success is undeserved, which breeds a compulsion to bring our outer reality into line with our inner one; so that we will end up being as unsuccessful as we feel.

In what ways have we perhaps self-sabotaged our lives at different points?

....

....

....

....

....

....

....

What can be hard to bear about happiness or success?

....

....

....

....

....

....

....

....

12   You as a colleague

All of us are, in some ways, difficult to have as colleagues. We bring certain emotional and psychological dynamics to play in group office life that makes things a bit harder than they should be. Perhaps we have tendencies to grow rather defensive when we're criticised, or we can't trust others, and so work around them, agreeing with their ideas to their faces, then doing something else behind their backs.

In what ways are you a difficult colleague to have?

....

....

....

....

....

....

....

....

....

....

What in your past might have contributed to your tricky sides?

....

....

....

....

....

....

....

....

....

....

13 Procrastination

What are you holding off from doing?

(Procrastination looks like laziness. It is, in fact, most often a species of fear.)

....
....
....
....
....
....
....
....
....
....
....
....
....
....
....
....
....
....
....
....
....
....
....
....
....
....
....

14 Feeling a failure

Our sense of success or failure is at heart extremely personal. Hence the powerful phenomenon of people who outwardly look very successful actually thinking they have wasted their lives (and, more cheerfully, vice versa).

Where do your ideas of success come from?

....

....

....

....

Do you actually believe in them, or merely subscribe to them?

....

....

....

....

What is it to be a winner?

....

....

....

....

What is a loser?

....

....

....

....

How might you reform your ideas of who is a loser and who is a winner?

....

....

....

....

15 Expenditure

There are so many things we are meant to buy and do in order to seem respectable or plain normal.

What are the expensive things we've spent money on that we don't, in our hearts, actually think delivered much pleasure?

....
....
....
....
....
....
....
....
....
....

What are the cheap things that are to hand that we, privately, think are extremely enjoyable and important?

....
....
....
....
....
....
....
....
....
....

16   Varieties of success

The word 'success' has a uniform, monolithic quality, being associated with money and status – and perhaps admiring articles in the newspaper as well. But 'success' only really means, in essence, doing something well. We might be a success at looking after children, or at remaining calm; at being a friend or reading good books.

How might these people variously define success? What useful things might they be picking up on?

A grandfather

....
....
....

A cancer patient

....
....
....

A four-year-old child

....
....
....
....

Define an alternative vision of success, one that appeals directly to you instead of what society expects of you.

....
....
....
....
....
....
....

17   The funeral

It is not an original point, but then again, nor is dying.

At the end, at the graveside, what do you want them to think?

....
....
....
....
....
....
....
....
....
....
....

And who is the 'them' that counts here?

....
....
....
....
....
....
....
....
....
....
....
....
....

6
Utopia

1   The Idea of utopia

We might dismiss thinking about how things should ideally be as mere fantasy, embarrassingly disconnected from reality. But asking about the best versions of things – the versions that strike us as most appealing – is a way of getting to know parts of our own minds. In considering the Utopian version of things, we're trying to tease out our own ideas of pleasure, beauty, happiness and what's properly interesting to us.

Suppose you were designing a hotel. Start with things you haven't enjoyed as much as you'd hoped, with things that were disappointing or frustrating, in the hotels you've stayed in before.

This is one of the most expensive
hotel rooms in the world.

But perhaps you might enjoy something more like
the bedroom of the philosopher Friedrich Nietzsche,
in Sils Maria in Switzerland.

In your ideal world, what would hotel bedrooms be like?

....

....

....

....

....

What about the rest of the hotel: What kind of interaction might you have with the person who cleans the room? Would you never see them? Would you get to know about their life?

....

....

....

....

....

....

How could you help families staying there have an interesting time together?

....

....

....

....

....

....

Would guests share a social life? What would be the best version of that for you?

....

....

....

....

....

2 Utopian travel

Let's turn to travel more generally.

In what ways have your holidays perhaps not been as fulfilling as you'd hoped?

....
....
....
....
....
....
....
....
....
....
....

What famous things you'd come to see were not as great as was suggested? Why?

....
....
....
....
....
....
....
....
....
....
....
....
....

What about the moments you really liked... even if they sound a bit strange: perhaps it was a time you were able to spend a few hours on your own or some music the taxi driver was playing or a compliment someone paid you about your hair?

....
....
....
....
....
....
....
....
....

Given all this, how would you get a holiday to go better? Be as weird as you like. It might mean staying at home. Or it could mean spending huge amounts on certain things (maybe a helicopter ride over a harbour would change your view of life) or spending much less (you might have a better time lodging in a family's spare bedroom than in a junior suite).

....
....
....
....
....
....
....
....
....
....
....

3   Utopian social life

We tend to accept the rules of social life we grow up with. But the rules of social life change throughout history and are, perhaps, amenable to further modification. In the 18th century, particularly in the salons of Paris, there was a view that social life should be focused around intellectually purposeful (but witty) conversation; a social evening should focus on a particular topic, which guests would be expected to think about beforehand – and ideally polish a few pertinent aphorisms to display to their friends.

In early 19th-century Germany, groups of friends used to gather in the evening, ideally around a large circular table, not to talk, but to get on with their own activities (knitting, reading, drawing, doing the household accounts, catching up on their correspondence) in a congenial atmosphere. It was about togetherness, not chat.

In early 20th-century England, the parties of the Bloomsbury Group were designed to prevent large groups of people talking; they favoured one-to-one conversations and arranged chairs and little tables in an attempt to ensure this would happen. Incidentally, they also particularly liked inviting ex-partners. They felt that if you'd had a relationship with someone you should make sure they stayed your friend afterwards.

In the past (though much less so nowadays), academics in a college would dine together almost every evening; the idea was that social life should be educational – you should expand your mind by continual contact with people who had expertise in other fields than your own. A physicist should regularly meet a historian; an expert in the politics of South America should often be exposed to the mind of someone who knows a lot about Norwegian poetry.

What tends to go wrong in your social life – things that aren't as much fun, or as rewarding, as they are theoretically meant to be (parties you didn't really enjoy; dinners where the conversation never took off...)?

....

....

....

....

....

....

....

....

....

....

....

Construct your ideal image of social life:

....

....

....

....

....

....

....

....

....

....

....

....

....

....

4   Utopian marriage

Marriage as we practise it today is at best 250 years old, a fusion of Romantic love, a philosophy of passion and adherence to bourgeois values around household management and sobriety. How might you redesign marriage?

How would people meet?

....

....

....

....

....

What would be the relationship between love and sex?

....

....

....

....

....

How would childcare work?

....

....

....

....

....

What role might friends and the community play?

....

....

....

....

....

5   Utopian cities

We all know that cities are nowadays far too expensive... but what do you think about the scale of buildings and streets, the architectural styles and the life at ground level?

Think of three cities you've really liked: what do they get right?

....
....
....
....
....
....
....
....
....
....
....
....
....
....
....
....
....
....
....
....
....
....

In Venice, over centuries, the idea evolved of grouping every small neighbourhood around a central square – just big enough to hold the few hundred people who lived nearby, but small enough that from an upper window you could (on a quiet afternoon) call over to your child playing with their friends on the other side.

In 17th-century Scotland, particularly in Edinburgh, it was believed that the rich and poor should live in different parts of the same building. Typically, the well-to-do would occupy larger flats or apartments on the lower floors and the less well off would live in smaller rooms on the upper floors: it ensured that everyone could be aware of each other's lives.

In Berlin in the 19th-century, very modest apartments were grouped together around courtyards and given splendid, highly dignified fronts towards the street. The idea was that you should have the right to live in a gracious building – even if you occupied only a tiny corner of it.

The 20th-century English writer Cyril Connolly believed that an ideal city was one you could walk out of, into real countryside, in an afternoon.

What do you think the ideal city would be like?

6   Utopian education

We have all sat through so many hours in mediocre education systems, we probably have some fascinating thoughts about how education could be improved.

In Ancient Greece, the philosopher Aristotle had a particularly ambitious idea of education. He held that most of the admirable human qualities were inherently learnable and teachable. In his ideal educational scheme, the task of teaching is to give us training to be nice and decent people, not merely productive and lucrative ones.

In 18th-century France, Jean-Jacques Rousseau argued that a crucial test of good education was whether or not it prepares us properly for a loving adult relationship.

In 19th-century England, the poet and educationalist Matthew Arnold argued that education was the key factor in allowing democracy to function well. He was particularly keen that schools should train pupils to listen carefully to views they didn't like and to accept compromise as an unavoidable part of life.

What didn't go right for you in your education?

....
....
....
....
....

Were you well prepared for the difficulties you've faced in adult life?

....
....
....
....
....

More generally, do you think education serves your society well? How might current education not be quite right for society in general, or for the whole world?

....
....
....
....
....

Are there things we're not being taught that we should be? Or are there things we are being taught that don't seem right or helpful? What do we need to know to be well-functioning adults? How could education help us be wiser, kinder and more resilient – as well as better informed?

....
....
....
....
....

7   Utopian media

In ancient Rome, the poet Ovid argued that the true goal of public speech (or the media) is to entertain us while instructing us. He was helpfully pessimistic about the human reluctance to be taught things – though he was deeply convinced that there's a huge amount we need to learn. On the other hand, he looked without too much dread at our strong natural inclination to entertainment. He dreamed of combining the two. The most important ideas should – with immense skill and wit – be made hugely entertaining. We'd become wiser without effort.

The German poet, dramatist and statesman Johann Wolfgang von Goethe lamented the way the press (which was then coming into existence) was dominated by people who don't themselves have experience of, or properly appreciate, the difficulties of government. It's easy, he felt, to say that another person is doing things badly, that they are exercising power stupidly, that they've come up with bad policies – because that's usually true. The problem is that it turns out to be fiendishly difficult to do better. He was beyond question one of the most intelligent and industrious people of the era and deeply conscious that, despite all the merits of his mind, his deep integrity and best application, he had made decisions that turned out, in retrospect, to be very unfortunate.

In the middle of the 20th century, the first director of the BBC, Lord Reith, took the view that the purpose of a national broadcaster was to elevate the nation. He thought that the authority and reach that comes from being a national broadcaster should be used to gently but persistently improve the taste and the minds of the entire population.

What are the less admirable features of the media, in your view?

....

....

....

....

....

....

....

....

....

....

....

....

What would the media be like if you were in charge? What kind of stories might
lead? What would their tone be like?

....

....

....

....

....

....

....

....

....

....

....

7
Culture

1   My canon

Without trying too hard to get it just right (you can always come back later and refine the list), note down a few things that appeal to you...

Works of art, paintings, sculpture:

....
....
....
....
....
....

Clothes:

....
....
....
....
....
....

Books:

....
....
....
....
....
....

Music:

....
....
....
....
....
....

Films:

....
....
....
....
....
....

Nature (a view, a tree, an animal):

....
....
....
....
....
....

Buildings:

....
....
....
....
....
....

Interiors:

....
....
....
....
....
....

Cities:

....
....
....
....
....
....

Pieces of furniture:

....
....
....
....
....
....

2   Culture and balance

We like (or dislike) things in culture without necessarily being able to tell ourselves exactly why. A big idea is that we seek in art what we don't have quite enough of in our lives. Around culture, we're often drawn to things that compensate us for what we lack internally.

Look at the two images opposite.

Is there one you are more drawn to?

....

....

....

....

....

....

....

....

....

What does your taste in art suggest you are missing in your life? (options include calm, fun, playfulness, luxury, nature, history...)

....

....

....

....

....

....

....

....

....

....

An emphatically tranquil, ordered and
abstract environment

An emphatically noisy and
busy environment

3   Memory

Works of art are tools for helping us do something we'd otherwise find difficult. One key problem we have is that our minds are leaky – we forget important things. Not so much passwords or appointments but emotions. We forget what's nice about someone (because we're often alerted to their defects), so it's useful to have a photo of them at their best to remind us. We forget important insights we once had. We lose touch with our own best moments of generosity and tenderness. Ideally we'd find a way of preserving them – of bottling them so we could have access to them when we need them. Up to now this bottling function, or preserving of experience so that we can remember it, has been performed on our behalf by artists. Monet didn't want to forget how he felt about sunlight on water or fog drifting over a river; Chardin wanted to preserve the emotions he had towards simple, homely scenes.

Select, almost at random, some object or work of art that you like (it doesn't need to be an absolute favourite). It could be a building near where you work or a song you sometimes find yourself humming.

....
....
....
....

What mood does it capture? Does it bring to mind a particular period of your life? What does it make you think of? Does it remind you of someone?

....
....
....
....

What might you be in danger of forgetting?

....
....
....
....
....

4   Consolation

Consolation invites us to look with tenderness on the generic sorrows of
humanity of which we have, in time, been allotted our necessary share.
Consolation aspires to turn rage and confusion into mourning and melancholy.
Our suffering is given back its proper level of dignity: our sorrows are not only
the result of our peculiar failings but part of the universal human condition. The
20th-century American artist Mark Rothko once stated that he wanted to make
art in which 'the sorrow in me, meets the sorrow in you.'

What works do you find consoling?

....
....
....
....
....
....
....
....
....
....

What do they console you for?

....
....
....
....
....
....
....
....
....
....
....
....

5   My musical axe

Franz Kafka thought that an important function of art, music or literature is to be 'an axe that breaks the frozen sea within us'. We carry around deep emotions that often don't make it to the surface in our crowded, practical lives. There are feelings that don't get much encouragement from the people we spend time around. But a song might pick up on them and amplify them. A euphoric burst of music seeks out and pushes forward a faint (but wonderful) feeling that we could love the whole world and be truly happy with our lives.

Give examples of music that, for you, work like an 'axe'?

....

....

....

....

....

....

....

....

....

....

What is liberated in you by this music?

....

....

....

....

....

....

....

....

....

....

6   Crying with art

Sometimes we weep with art not when things are horrible but when they are almost unbearably lovely – which stands in precise and powerful contrast to the way our life has been very difficult. We might melt when, in a story, a rather distant father finally turns shyly to his son and begins to say, with deep embarrassment but very real emotion, how sorry he is: it's showing us, perhaps, what we secretly long for but cannot seem to achieve properly for ourselves. We're glimpsing the beautiful ideal from which at the moment we feel excluded. Or maybe we find we're holding back tears when a character who has reason to be angry turns out to be forgiving and generous. We cry because we're recognising a concentrated moment of intense goodness.

When have you been moved to tears by a scene in a film or a book?

....
....
....
....
....
....
....
....
....

Can you identify what harshness in your life made the goodness in the art stand out?

....
....
....
....
....
....
....
....
....

7   Me as a plate

One of the less obvious but powerful things that objects do is sum up various aspects of who we are. When we see a room or a pair of shoes or a plate or a car we can form a quick mental sketch of the kind of person it is like – the kind of person who would want to own this thing and would identify strongly with it. And sometimes that person will be us. At points, we're hitting upon objects that speak of our character or values. They externalise certain parts of who we are. And this is very useful – because some of the nicer things about us are not always on display or they might not be particularly obvious to others. When we're buying things we're often trying to answer the underlying question: who am I in this area?; what kind of garden chair is 'me'?; what sort of cutlery is in tune with my personality? Who am I in the world of lampshades or bathroom tiles?

List your favourite objects and why you are like them.

Lamp:

....

Car:

....

Plate:

....

Fork:

....

Chair:

....

Cup:

....

Other:

....

8   Clothes

The fashion industry can certainly have silly aspects. But in general we take clothes quite seriously. We're conscious that in some way or another it matters how we dress. We're sending signals to the world (and to ourselves) about who we are, or who we're not, or about who we'd like to be or would like to be thought to be.

Importantly, there might be anxieties we're trying to ward off through our choice of shoes or of a jacket. We're trying through our choices to fend off the prejudices and false judgements of others.

Who would you like people to think you are via your taste in clothes?

....

....

....

....

....

....

....

....

....

What judgements or prejudices are you trying to ward off through your choice of clothes?

....

....

....

....

....

....

....

....

....

....

9   Works of art as yet uncreated

Despite all the art already created, we might not yet have encountered in culture the things we most want to meet. For instance, we might read a novel with a tragic ending and think that it's a pity it didn't have a happier resolution. We're starting to imagine the kind of art we personally want. Maybe we'd love to hear a song in the style of ABBA but not about love, more about the difficulty of being a parent of small children. We might think it would be nice if an airport terminal looked more like a Gothic cathedral.

At this point, our internal censor might get very critical and think we're stupid or insane. But every work of art started with someone wanting to put forward an idea that mattered to them, or create things that they liked. An artist is someone who is more devoted (than we usually are) to making things they delight in and has asked themselves a little more insistently: what do I personally want from a work of art?

If you could tweak, rearrange or invent from scratch (and without having the slightest worry about how realistic it would be, whether it would be popular or acclaimed) what would you really like in:

A novel

....

....

....

....

....

....

A film

....

....

....

....

....

A house for you

....

....

....

....

....

....

Music

....

....

....

....

....

A shopping centre

....

....

....

....

....

A train station

....

....

....

....

....

....

8
Sorrow
& Compassion

1   My sorrows

It can seem odd to consider the pity we deserve. There's often an instinctive distrust of 'feeling sorry for oneself'. And yet we are often properly entitled to a significant dose of self-compassion. Our lives are essentially difficult. So many things go wrong: we live with regrets, unfulfilled hopes; stressful relationships or loneliness; we try hard and yet don't seem to make progress; our ideas aren't understood by others; the city and country we are in is badly run. There's so much that we could wish different in ourselves, our past, others and the wider world. But our capacity to change these things often looks minimal or non-existent.

What have been and are your sorrows around:

Parents

....

....

....

....

....

Love

....

....

....

....

....

Children

....

....

....

....

....

....

Friends

....
....
....
....

Money

....
....
....
....

Work

....
....
....
....

Health

....
....
....
....

Society

....
....
....
....

2   Guilt

There are powerful, profound times when we fully and seriously acknowledge something that is fundamentally difficult: we aren't very nice people. Not in every way, but just in some important respects. We're inwardly admitting our failings with regard to ourselves and other people. We've let others down. We've been unfair – we've said some mean things about someone who doesn't deserve such a brutal assessment. We've wished ill of someone who has done nothing worse than happen to be in competition with us for a contract or a position. We've ignored someone who was only looking for a kind word from us; we've criticised harshly (in a way we'd deeply resent if it were turned on us); we've lusted after people who might be horrified to hear of our imaginings; we've lost our temper over minor things; we've blamed others when really it was our own fault (as we knew even at the time in a small corner of our minds); we've betrayed confidences; we've exaggerated our own status or importance…

Feeling guilty isn't at all nice and it doesn't sound very impressive. But it usefully counteracts a deep-set tendency: to blame others, to insist that nothing wrong is ever our fault; to get away with whatever we can. We're momentarily dropping our defensive guard. We're taking our place in the world as genuinely responsible adults who recognise a central but melancholy fact: that we too are sinners: that the troubles of existence are not only the work of others; that we are flawed. That we can be genuinely sorry and ashamed; that we may need to say (and with justice) an abject 'sorry' and hope that another will find the generosity to forgive us.

It's not a unique accusation. Everyone has done so much that ideally they wouldn't have. Everyone has much to apologise for.

What do you feel guilty about?

....
....
....
....
....
....

What would you, in retrospect, have done differently?

....
....
....
....
....
....

Who have you hurt? Whose life have you made more difficult (even if you didn't mean to)?

....
....
....
....
....
....

Whose forgiveness do you long for?

....
....
....
....
....

3   The pin

When a person is behaving badly, we should always strive to look for, or at least imagine, 'the pin': a jabbing object we can't easily see but that must be there, disturbing them, hurting them, driving them wild. We might never quite know what the pin is, but there wouldn't be so much bad temper without it. If someone had a strong physical pain, we'd totally understand that they might scream and shout and be incredibly impatient, or incapable of taking an interest in the anecdote we're telling them about what we did on Saturday. When we can see an obvious source of pain, we instantly understand and forgive unappealing conduct.

In a non-physical sense, what pins might others around us have?

....

....

....

....

We don't actually know what people's pins are: they mostly don't tell us; it's not immediately obvious; the pin may be very carefully concealed. Others may look strong and secure, they may seem confident and competent. But it is almost certain there is a pin there, because the background, wise assumption is that no one can make it into adult life without suffering some serious inner wounds. Whenever we get to know a person really well, we always get some idea. They never feel they can live up to the expectations of a demanding parent; they feel guilty for something that happened long ago but that still haunts their imagination; they always fear they are on the verge of being humiliated; there's a deep but secret sorrow in their relationship; they are desperately worried about their health; they suffer from insomnia; they have strange nightmares; they don't believe anyone can genuinely like them; they are depressed.

And your pins: what are the private points of suffering in your life that others don't know about?

....

....

....

....

....

4   In what ways am I crazy?

It's one of the most important admissions we can make: that we are in fact in some ways rather mad – disturbed, weird, impossible. But it's a closely guarded secret. We can't easily imagine other people hearing about this and not recoiling in disgust. The ideal person you could tell would be someone who had heard this kind of admission from many others, who would not be in the least surprised or shocked; perhaps they would have guessed long ago that something like this would be true of you because they had enough experience of the secrets of others to know exactly what to expect. They wouldn't betray us; they wouldn't tell anyone; they wouldn't use it against us; they would be compassionate; they would understand the burden we were carrying. And they would be alive to their own zones of extreme oddity. They wouldn't try to fix us immediately or brusquely. They would just listen and be kind.

What would you tell such a person about yourself?

....

....

....

....

....

....

....

....

....

....

....

....

....

....

....

....

....

....

5   Treating others like children

A significant portion of life is passed being irritated, disappointed and frustrated with other people. We are appalled by their conduct, saddened by their attitudes and furious with the stupid things they're always doing. But there's one group of people around whom this rarely or never happens: young children. They behave in ways that are objectively awful: they throw away something you've just given them; they scream when they don't get what they want; they blame you for things that can't possibly be your fault. But we tend to remain smiling and sweet because we understand: of course – they are children. We interpret the child's behaviour very charitably – and accurately. We keep in mind that their emotions are far stronger than their powers of reason; they are easily frightened and can't properly separate imagination from reality; and they aren't easily capable of seeing things from our point of view. We understand that if they are feeling hungry or tired or cold it's going to show up in bouts of troublesome behaviour. We don't think they are bad or wicked or selfish.

Something very similar applies to adults. Although they're physically larger and know a lot of things and can perhaps drive a car or write a business report, much of adults' emotional equipment is shared with children. It can sound a touch patronising but it is actually an act of immensely helpful generosity if we can see others as big children.

Behaviour	If an adult did this, I'd think...	If a child did this, I'd think...
Tell a lie		
Distract me while I'm driving		
Say they hate what I've made for dinner		
Ignore me when I ask a question		
Make a terrible mess in the living room		

9
Re-enchantment

1   Small pleasures

We frequently associate pleasure with special things: we seek out elements that are rare, expensive or famous. Our ideas of what might make for a good holiday often reflect this system of ideas. It's thrilling to drink a famous brand of champagne or to see one of the most famous works of art in the world; we're excited to hear that a celebrity is coming to a party we're going to. There's nothing inherently wrong with these enjoyments. The problem is that they are unlikely to come our way very often. They target only a very small range of opportunities.

A useful alternative is to think about what might be called 'small pleasures': things that look minor, don't have any glamour attached to them and may happen quite often: eating a piece of fruit, having a bath, whispering in bed in the dark, talking to a grandparent, or scanning through old photos of when you were a child... But these pleasures may be just as intense and precious to us as their more celebrated counterparts. They can be among the most moving and satisfying we can have. But we don't always latch onto them properly, or give them full appreciation, because they don't (as yet) enjoy a high level of public endorsement.

It might take some time to gradually build up a list of your own small pleasures. Because almost by definition we tend not to pay them all that much attention: sorting socks after the wash; watching one's own shadow; feeling tired after having worked well and hard, the second bite of a toasted cheese sandwich... In fact, our lives are filled with less well-identified satisfactions and lovely experiences that we haven't fully latched onto. A list is important because it provides a crucial counter-argument to our natural attention to the more troubling and gloomy sides of our existence.

List your own 'small pleasures':

....
....
....
....
....
....
....
....
....
....
....
....
....
....
....
....
....
....
....
....
....
....
....
....
....
....
....
....
....

2   Water towers

People thought water towers were boring and ugly – until artists started looking at them.

Starting in 1972, a German couple – Bernd and Hilla Becher – began photographing water towers in various countries. The structures were often regarded as ungainly eyesores. But by looking at them long and carefully, the Bechers discovered the less obvious, but real, charm and even the peculiar beauty of these highly utilitarian buildings. The Bechers were making a fundamental artistic move. They were devoting attention and tenderness to things that are usually overlooked – and in the process discovering a new realm of pleasure and interest. Of course, it's not actually necessary to be a recognised artist to do this. It's a universal capacity of which we can always make use.

What's your possible equivalent of the towers? Are there things you could try out liking? It doesn't have to be things most people ignore, only things that you tend to rush past: perhaps the faces of older people, paving stones, electricity pylons, petrol stations… The experiment won't always work, but it might sometimes. If you were your own version of the Bechers, what might you photograph?

....

....

....

....

....

....

....

....

....

....

....

....

....

....

3   Sublime moments

We sometimes use 'sublime' just to say that something is very nice. But it has an older and deeper meaning. Traditionally, in philosophy, sublime means an experience that hugely (if briefly) expands our sense of ourselves in a very interesting way. When looking up at the stars at night, for instance, we might be struck by how incomprehensibly vast the universe is and how tiny we are in a physical sense. But at the same time our mind – or spirit, if we like this word – seems to expand to meet the immense grandeur of the heavens. Our immediate local worries drop away, we're conscious of the vast sweep of time and of the universality of our experience: since the earliest humans, people have been amazed (we can easily feel) by the same sight. We're tapping into something elemental and we feel uplifted by it.

What things, across your life, can you recall that have triggered this kind of feeling in you?

....

....

....

....

....

....

....

....

Can you start to put into words how you felt at those times?

....

....

....

....

....

....

....

....

4   My genius

It's not an arrogant assertion – and it's likely to be true, however modest and frankly dull we often feel. The term 'genius', which might be justified for Picasso, Einstein or Virginia Woolf, feels exceptionally remote from the everyday workings of our minds. But there is a radically different view, suggested by a hugely prescient quote from the 19th-century American genius Ralph Waldo Emerson: 'In the minds of geniuses, we find – once more – our own neglected thoughts.' What he's getting at is deeply poignant. Often enough we touch upon insights that are in the same zone as the ideas of the genius. Taken seriously, developed rigorously, expanded and refined, our ideas too could sometimes be genuinely and impressively important to others. It's not that we don't have the initial notion; it's just that – as Emerson puts it – we neglect these half-formed starting points. It's not usually laziness. It's often, curiously, our own modesty that gets in the way. We assume from the start (quite wrongly) that what we think can't be important. Or fear gets in the way. If we push an idea seriously, if we cultivate it and develop it, we start to think things that initially look very odd.

It's a difficult question to ask, but what are the ideas of your own – the passing thoughts, the stray observations – that potentially could be developed? What are the thoughts that you are neglecting?

....

....

....

....

....

....

....

....

....

....

....

(It's so tricky because we don't notice our negligence. It feels normal and almost inevitable. And yet it isn't really inevitable. It may take a long time to build up even a short list. And that's not odd or worrying. Because the development of a handful of genius thoughts of one's own might be the work of a lifetime.)

5 Being silly

Our dignity is – rightly – very important to us. It's a huge achievement to be able to present oneself as a moderately realistic, reasonable, fairly industrious, self-controlled adult. But it comes at a special price. We've had to squash the undignified, silly, childish, naughty, ridiculous aspects of our own nature. Being silly isn't really silly. Especially if we can be silly in the company of another competent adult. We can like throwing water bombs out of windows and responsibly share the burden of a home loan; we can hold down a very sensible job and enjoy bouncing on a sofa. We're exploring the basis of the human condition: we are both absurd and rational; wise and foolish; grown-up and rather childish. And we need to know this not only about ourselves but about other people as well.

What kinds of silliness did you relish as a child?

....
....
....
....
....
....
....
....

What things might you like to do now that you'd possibly feel embarrassed to admit because they seem a touch infantile? How much scope do you currently give to the sillier aspects of who you are?

....
....
....
....
....
....
....
....

6   Humour

Life is full of annoying, frustrating and bemusing things and we tend to take
this as a reason to feel either angry or melancholy. Strikingly, though, much of
the most hilarious comedy in the world builds on precisely such experiences.
The jokes we love and the comedies we find entertaining start with situations
that could otherwise be seen as horrible. In a film we can laugh at someone's
incredibly inappropriate comment – though if we did this ourselves we'd be only
ashamed and if our partner said the same thing we'd probably get immensely
irked. If we go on holiday and the hotel is a bit of a disaster we feel furious;
we've been cheated. But to a comedy sketch writer this is a deeply fascinating
moment: it might be the seed of a riotous series.

Think of some of the more annoying things that have happened to you recently
– a maddening misunderstanding, a stupid delay, losing a key document, saying
something embarrassing… and imagine it from the point of view of a stand-up
comic. They're going to retell this as an entertaining moment of universal human
comedy. We won't get it to a perfectly polished state. But we're doing something
more important. We're starting to imagine what it would be like to laugh at
things that usually only drive us mad.

7   Nature

When the human world disappoints, it's not unusual to turn to nature. But what specifically is it about nature that offers us consolation?

To the Stoic philosophers of Ancient Rome, it was the idea of inevitability – so explicit in the natural world – that appealed: the tide has to rise and fall according to the phases of the moon; the bough of the tree has to bend when the wind blows; the lion has to hunt the gazelle. The swallow has to migrate. The laws of nature are fixed by forces no-one chooses but to which everything must submit. It is a strange relief to remind ourselves that broadly the same kind of inevitability applies in our own lives as well.

During the Tang dynasty, the Chinese poet Bai Juyi as he got older felt increasingly excluded from what he called 'the world of youngsters': he turned instead to nature for companionship. In one poem he writes:

> Turning my head around, I ask the pair of rocks:
> 'Can you keep company with an old man like myself?'
> Although the rocks cannot speak,
> They promise that we will be three friends.

He sought out oddly-shaped, exposed rocks that had been dramatically weathered and eroded: time had made them more interesting.

A dog may love us quite independently of our merits or failings as perceived by the human community. They may want a great deal from us – endless throwings of sticks and pattings of heads – but they are indifferent to almost everything else about us. They don't care how the work meeting went or how our bank account is looking or whether we did well in an exam. They invite us into a world in which it is impossible to acquire status or meet with disgrace on any of these counts.

In what ways, similar or different, does nature appeal to you?

10
Conclusion

1   My coat of arms

Traditionally, aristocratic families would have a coat of arms, painted onto a shield or carved above the fireplace in the hall.

Using a system of symbols, the coat of arms says who your ancestors were; it might make reference to the origins of the family in some long-past heroic event; it signals what other families you are allied with and what your status is. If other people know this, they will be able to interact properly with you.

It sounds odd, initially, but we need our own version of this. We too need to alert others to important things about us – other people can't be relied upon to find it all out for themselves; we have to let them know and ideally in a rapid way. It's just that the facts and details we need to communicate are rather different.

Looking back over this book, imagine what you would most like to pick out to define to others who you truly are. Fill in this blank coat of arms, finding symbols to represent ideas.

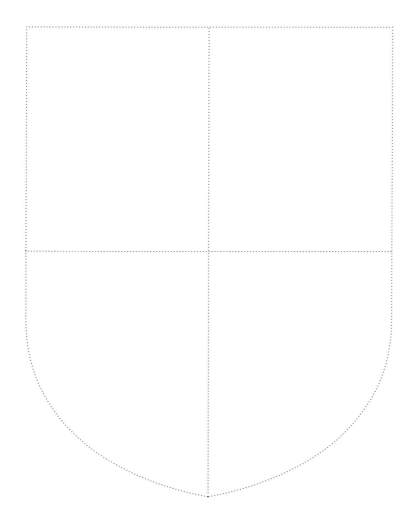

Notes

Perhaps almost all the problems in the world derive, ultimately, from our collective inability to explain frankly to ourselves and to each other who we really are. We get preoccupied by what people are supposed to be like, rather than what we and they are really like. It's tantalising: if we could bear to show each other a more accurate self-portrait, we'd have fewer illusions, more compassion, less frustration and more love in our lives and in our world.